Finding Liberation: A Guide to Releasing Attachments to People

Table of Contents

Introduction

In the tapestry of our lives, relationships are the threads that weave together moments of joy, connection, and shared experiences. They can be the source of profound love, support, and understanding, enriching our existence in immeasurable ways. Yet, like any tapestry, relationships can also fray and unravel, leaving us with the threads of attachment that tug at our hearts and souls long after the connection has dissolved.

"Finding Liberation: A Guide to Releasing Attachments to People" is an exploration of the complex and often challenging journey of letting go. It is a journey that all of us, at some point in our lives, must undertake. Whether it's the end of a romantic partnership, the detachment from a toxic relationship, or the evolution of a friendship, the process of releasing attachments is a fundamental aspect of our human experience.

This book delves into the intricate tapestry of human connections and the powerful emotions that accompany them. It is a guide for those who find themselves at the crossroads of attachment, yearning for the freedom and clarity that come with letting go. It is a companion for those who seek to navigate the delicate balance between love and liberation.

Throughout these pages, we will embark on a journey of self-discovery and growth. We will explore the art of setting boundaries, the profound act of forgiveness, the transformative power of self-care, and the intricate dance of navigating relationships with grace. We will delve into the depths of grief and loss, finding solace in the healing process, and emerge on the other side with renewed strength and resilience.

"Finding Liberation" is not just a guide; it is a testament to the resilience of the human spirit. It is a celebration of the profound potential for personal growth and transformation that arises from the ashes of attachment. It is an acknowledgment that letting go is not the end but the beginning of a new chapter filled with possibilities, self-discovery, and healthier, more fulfilling connections.

As we journey together through the following chapters, may you find solace in knowing that you are not alone in your quest for liberation. May you discover the tools and insights needed to release attachments, heal from the past, and embrace a future filled with the promise of authentic, meaningful relationships. "Finding

Liberation" is your guide, your companion, and your beacon of hope on this transformative journey.

Navigating Relationships with Grace

In the realm of releasing attachments to people, this chapter serves as a crucial prologue. It is the preliminary step before diving into the depths of connection and detachment, a prerequisite that lays the groundwork for a healthy and balanced approach to relationships. It underscores the significance of understanding what a healthy relationship entails and the effort required to maintain it.

Navigating relationships with grace begins with self-awareness. Individuals embarking on this journey must first understand themselves, their values, needs, and boundaries. This self-awareness forms the bedrock upon which they can build healthy connections. It enables them to enter relationships with clarity about who they are and what they seek in a partner, friend or relative, reducing the likelihood of settling for less than they deserve.

Healthy relationships are not solely defined by the blissful moments of togetherness but also by the way people navigate challenges and conflicts. It's the recognition that relationships will inevitably encounter rough waters, and the measure of their strength lies in how they weather those storms. Navigating relationships with grace means embracing conflicts as opportunities for growth, learning to communicate effectively, and approaching disagreements with empathy and respect.

It involves setting and respecting boundaries. In healthy relationships, individuals honor each other's personal space, needs, and autonomy. This mutual respect creates a safe and nurturing environment where both partners can flourish as individuals while growing together as a couple. It also ensures that relationships are not built on codependency but on interdependence, where both individuals contribute to each other's well-being without losing their sense of self.

Navigating relationships with grace requires patience and a commitment to the long haul. It's an understanding that the initial sparks of friendship or romance may give way to deeper, more profound connections over time. It's the willingness to invest time and effort into the relationship, recognizing that it will evolve and change as both individuals grow and evolve.

Navigating relationships with grace is the essential preamble to the journey of releasing attachments to people. It's about understanding what constitutes a healthy relationship, embracing the effort required to sustain it, and laying a strong foundation for the challenges and joys that lie ahead. It's a journey that begins with self-awareness, empathy, respect, and a deep commitment to nurturing connections that enrich our lives.

Understanding Healthy Relationships

Intricate dynamics form the foundation of meaningful human connections. Healthy relationships are not mere chance occurrences; they are nurtured and cultivated through mutual respect, open communication, and genuine care for one another. At their core, these relationships are built on a solid framework of trust, the cornerstone that upholds the entire structure. Trust is not easily given but is something that is earned over time, as we demonstrate our reliability, consistency, and honesty in our interactions with one another.

Effective communication is another key element in healthy relationships. It's not just about talking but also about truly listening to one another. In these relationships, people feel comfortable expressing their thoughts, feelings, and concerns without fear of judgment. This open exchange of ideas fosters understanding and empathy, paving the way for conflict resolution and compromise when differences arise.

Healthy relationships are characterized by shared values, interests, and goals. While individuality is celebrated, a sense of togetherness is also nurtured, creating a balance that allows each person to thrive while contributing to the growth and fulfillment of the partnership. In such relationships, there's an understanding that both parties are equal partners, with neither dominating nor being dominated.

Healthy relationships promote emotional well-being. They provide a safe space where individuals can be vulnerable, sharing their joys and sorrows without reservation. This emotional intimacy creates a deep sense of connection and support, enhancing the overall quality of life.

As we explore the dynamics of healthy relationships, it becomes evident that they require effort, patience, and a genuine desire to understand and connect with one another. They are a testament to the power of human connection, where two individuals come together, not to complete each other, but to complement and enhance one another's lives in a harmonious and fulfilling way.

Effective Communication

In the realm of releasing attachments to people, effective communication emerges as the cornerstone of healthy relationships. It is the lifeblood that courses through the veins of any meaningful connection, providing nourishment and sustenance. At its essence, effective communication is a two-way street—a dance where both partners take turns leading and following, sharing their inner worlds and listening to the melodies of each other's hearts.

In the world of healthy relationships, communication is not just about the words we choose but also the intention behind them. It's the art of conveying not only the content but also the emotions, thoughts, and vulnerabilities that reside within us. It involves speaking our truth with authenticity and integrity, revealing our fears and aspirations, and acknowledging the humanity in the person before us.

Listening, too, is a pivotal aspect of effective communication. It's not merely the act of hearing words but also the practice of active engagement with the speaker. In healthy relationships, listening goes beyond the surface level; it involves empathetic understanding, where we seek to comprehend not just what is said but also what is left unsaid. It's about tuning in to the subtle nuances of tone, body language, and context, grasping the full spectrum of the message being conveyed.

Conflict resolution is another facet of effective communication within healthy relationships. Disagreements and differences of opinion are inevitable, but in these relationships, they are viewed as opportunities for growth and understanding. Partners engage in constructive dialogue, seeking common ground and solutions that honor the needs and desires of both parties.

Transparency and honesty are the bedrock of effective communication. In these relationships, there is a commitment to truthfulness, even when the truth may be uncomfortable. Trust is cultivated through the consistency between words and actions, and partners rely on this trust to weather the storms that life may bring.

Moreover, healthy relationships acknowledge the power of non-verbal communication. Small gestures of love and affection, a comforting touch, a warm smile, and the language of the eyes speak volumes. These subtleties convey emotions that words alone cannot capture, deepening the connection between individuals.

In sum, effective communication in the context of releasing attachments to people is an art form that requires practice, patience, and a genuine willingness to connect. It is the medium through which intimacy is nurtured, conflicts are resolved, and bonds are strengthened. It is the bridge that spans the gap between two hearts, allowing them to traverse the journey of life together with empathy, understanding, and love.

Building Trust and Connection

In the journey of releasing attachments to people, building trust and connection is a foundational chapter that sets the stage for meaningful and sustainable relationships. Trust is the currency of human connection, the glue that binds individuals together in a web of mutual respect and understanding. It is not bestowed lightly but is rather a priceless gift that is earned through consistent actions and genuine intentions.

In the context of healthy relationships, trust is cultivated through a series of shared experiences. It begins with the small promises kept and the reliability demonstrated in everyday interactions. As individuals show up for one another, fulfilling commitments and being present both in times of joy and adversity, trust begins to take root. It deepens further as partners confide in each other, revealing their vulnerabilities and sharing their fears and hopes without reservation.

Trust is also closely intertwined with transparency and open communication. In these relationships, there is a commitment to honesty, where individuals speak their truth even when it is uncomfortable. This honesty is a testament to the depth of trust, as it acknowledges that trust can withstand the challenges of reality. It is not the absence of mistakes or misunderstandings but rather the willingness to address them openly and work through them together.

Vulnerability plays a significant role in building trust and connection. It is in moments of vulnerability that true intimacy is forged. When individuals allow themselves to be seen and known, warts and all, they create a space for their partners to do the same. This reciprocity of vulnerability deepens the connection, as it fosters empathy and a profound understanding of each other's inner worlds.

Building trust and connection is a gradual process that requires patience and a steadfast commitment to one another. It is not a one-time achievement but an ongoing endeavor that requires consistent effort and care. Trust is the bridge that allows individuals to venture into the depths of each other's souls, secure in the knowledge that they are held and cherished.

In conclusion, trust and connection are the lifeblood of healthy relationships. They are the fruits of shared experiences, open communication, vulnerability, and unwavering commitment. In releasing attachments to people, it is through the cultivation of trust and connection that individuals find solace and strength in each other's presence, embarking on a journey of profound connection and mutual growth.

Detaching from Toxic Relationships

Identifying Toxic Patterns

In the chapter on detaching from toxic relationships, we embark on the journey of recognizing and understanding the intricate web of toxic patterns that can entangle us in unhealthy connections. Toxic patterns are like invisible chains that bind us, often unnoticed until we begin to feel their weight. Identifying these patterns is the first step toward liberation and healing.

Toxic patterns can manifest in various ways. They may include manipulation, control, or emotional abuse. These behaviors can be subtle, often disguised as love or concern. Recognizing toxic patterns demands a keen awareness of the signs, such as feeling constantly criticized or belittled, experiencing a loss of self-esteem, or feeling anxious or fearful in the presence of the other person. It also involves acknowledging when a relationship becomes overwhelmingly draining, rather than a source of support and growth.

Moreover, toxic patterns can thrive on cycles of tension and relief. There may be moments of kindness or affection that temporarily alleviate the pain, creating confusion and ambivalence. It is essential to recognize that these sporadic moments of positivity do not negate the toxicity of the overall pattern.

Identifying toxic patterns also requires introspection. It involves examining our own behavior and responses within the relationship. Sometimes, we may unwittingly contribute to the toxicity by enabling or perpetuating harmful dynamics. Self-awareness is key to breaking free from this cycle.

Healthy boundaries play a pivotal role in identifying toxic patterns. It's about recognizing when our personal boundaries are crossed or violated and having the courage to assertively communicate and enforce those boundaries. It also involves acknowledging that we have the right to prioritize our well-being and mental health.

Identifying toxic patterns in the process of detaching from toxic relationships. It involves recognizing the subtle signs, understanding the dynamics at play, and taking a courageous stance to protect one's well-being. It is the first step toward breaking free from the grip of toxicity and embarking on a path of healing and self-discovery.

Setting Boundaries

With detaching from toxic relationships, the discussion naturally leads to the critical topic of setting boundaries. Boundaries are the invisible lines that delineate what is acceptable and unacceptable in any relationship. They serve as protective barriers, safeguarding our emotional and mental well-being. In toxic relationships, where these lines are often blurred or disregarded, learning to set and enforce boundaries becomes an indispensable skill for our own self-preservation.

Setting boundaries begins with self-awareness and self-respect. It necessitates a deep understanding of our own needs, values, and limits. It is about recognizing what makes us comfortable and uncomfortable, what feels respectful and disrespectful, and what aligns with our core values. These insights become the compass by which we navigate the terrain of our relationships.

Communicating boundaries is the next vital step. It involves expressing our needs and limits clearly and assertively to the other person. Effective boundary-setting requires open and honest communication, free from blame or judgment. It is not about controlling the other person but rather about articulating our expectations and advocating for our well-being. This can be a challenging process, especially in toxic relationships, where boundaries may have been consistently ignored or violated in the past.

Consistency is key when it comes to setting and maintaining boundaries. It's about reinforcing our limits through our actions. When a boundary is crossed, we must be prepared to follow through with the consequences we've communicated. This consistency helps establish a clear framework for the relationship, making it evident that our boundaries are non-negotiable.

In toxic relationships, setting boundaries can be met with resistance or pushback. The other person may react negatively, attempting to maintain the status quo. It is essential to stand firm and prioritize our well-being, even in the face of resistance. Over time, consistent boundary-setting can lead to a shift in the dynamics of the relationship.

Setting boundaries is an act of self-care and self-respect. It is about acknowledging that we have the right to protect our emotional and mental health. It is not selfish but rather a necessary step toward detaching from toxic relationships and creating space for healthier connections.

Seeking Support and Closure

Detaching from a toxic relationship can be a profoundly challenging and emotionally draining experience. It is a journey fraught with uncertainty, self-doubt, and a rollercoaster of emotions. Seeking support from trusted friends, family members, or a therapist is not a sign of weakness but a demonstration of self-compassion and wisdom.

Support can take various forms, from having a compassionate friend to confide in to seeking professional guidance from a therapist or counselor. These supportive individuals provide a safe space to express our feelings, thoughts, and fears without judgment. They offer validation and reassurance, reminding us that we are not alone in our struggles. Sharing our experiences can be cathartic and can help us gain clarity and perspective on the toxic relationship.

Therapy, in particular, can be invaluable in detaching from toxic relationships. A therapist can help us understand the underlying patterns and dynamics of the toxic relationship, explore our own role in it, and develop healthier coping strategies. They guide us in setting boundaries, building self-esteem, and processing the emotions that arise during the detachment process. Therapy offers a structured and professional approach to healing and recovery.

Closure is another essential aspect of detaching from toxic relationships. Closure is not always about receiving an apology or an explanation from the other person, as toxic individuals may not be willing or capable of providing that closure. Instead, closure is about finding internal resolution and acceptance. It involves recognizing that the toxic relationship has ended for a reason and that we are deserving of peace and healing.

Closure often requires letting go of resentment and anger, forgiving ourselves for any perceived shortcomings, and acknowledging the pain we have endured. It's about releasing the emotional attachment to the toxic person and choosing to focus on our own well-being and growth. Closure can be a gradual process, and it may involve rituals or symbolic gestures that help us symbolize the end of the toxic chapter in our lives.

Coping with the End of a Relationship

Processing Grief and Loss

The dissolution of a relationship, whether it was toxic or held deep emotional significance, can trigger a complex and challenging grieving process. It's essential to understand that grieving the end of a relationship is a natural and necessary part of healing.

Grief, in the context of relationship loss, is not limited to romantic partnerships but can extend to any meaningful connection, including friendships and family ties. The emotions that accompany this process are wide-ranging and can include sadness, anger, confusion, guilt, and even relief. These emotions may ebb and flow, appearing unexpectedly and with varying intensity.

Processing grief and loss begins with acknowledging these emotions without judgment. It is normal to experience a mix of conflicting feelings, and there is no "right" or "wrong" way to grieve. Embracing our emotions with compassion is an essential step toward healing.

As we navigate the grieving process, it is also essential to find healthy outlets for our emotions. This might involve talking to a trusted friend, journaling, or seeking the guidance of a therapist or counselor. Expressing our feelings can be cathartic and help us make sense of the complex emotions we are experiencing.

Self-care becomes paramount during this time. Nurturing our physical, emotional, and mental well-being is crucial. Engaging in activities that bring us joy and comfort, maintaining a balanced diet, getting regular exercise, and prioritizing sleep are essential components of self-care during the grieving process.

Another aspect of processing grief and loss involves reflecting on the lessons learned from the relationship. Every connection, even those that end, can offer valuable insights and personal growth opportunities. Examining what we have learned and how we have grown can help us find meaning and closure in the experience.

Time plays a significant role in the process of healing. Grief does not adhere to a set timetable, and it is different for everyone. It is essential to be patient with ourselves and allow the healing process to unfold at its own pace.

Moving Forward

With the end of a relationship, the pivotal phase of moving forward is where the focus shifts from the past to the present and the future. It is a phase that speaks to resilience, personal growth, and the process of rebuilding one's life after the emotional upheaval of a relationship's conclusion.

Moving forward begins with self-compassion. It entails acknowledging that the healing process is not linear and that setbacks and moments of sorrow may arise. It's about treating ourselves with the same kindness and understanding that we would offer to a dear friend facing a similar situation. Self-compassion provides a foundation of emotional support as we navigate the uncertainties of the post-relationship landscape.

One of the first steps in moving forward is rediscovering our sense of self. Relationships often involve a merging of identities, and it's common to lose sight of who we are as individuals. Reconnecting with our interests, passions, and goals allows us to rebuild our self-esteem and reaffirm our autonomy. It is an opportunity for self-discovery and personal growth.

Moving forward also involves reframing the narrative of the past. It's about examining the relationship and its ending from a perspective that emphasizes the lessons learned, the personal strengths gained, and the opportunities for growth that have emerged. This shift in perspective empowers us to extract meaning from the experience and find closure.

Healthy relationships with others also play a significant role in moving forward. Seeking the support of friends and loved ones provides a vital social network that can counter feelings of isolation and loneliness. These relationships offer a sense of belonging and remind us that we are not alone on our journey.

Forgiveness, both of the other person and ourselves, is a transformative aspect of moving forward. Forgiveness does not imply condoning hurtful actions or behaviors but rather releasing the emotional burden they carry. It is about freeing ourselves from the weight of resentment and anger, allowing us to move forward with a lighter heart.

Setting new goals and intentions is a tangible way to embrace the future. It might involve pursuing new interests, reinvigorating old ones, or setting professional and personal aspirations. These goals give us a sense of purpose and direction, fueling our motivation to move forward.

Moving forward encapsulates the essence of resilience and personal growth in the aftermath of a relationship's end. It is a chapter that celebrates self-compassion, self-discovery, and the profound capacity of the human spirit to heal and flourish. It reminds us that although the end of a relationship can be challenging, it also marks the beginning of a new chapter filled with possibilities for happiness, fulfillment, and healthier connections in the future.

Self-Care and Healing

In coping with the end of a relationship, the paramount themes of self-care and healing take center stage. This chapter delves into the importance of prioritizing one's emotional and mental well-being during the tumultuous aftermath of a relationship's conclusion. Self-care becomes a lifeline, and healing becomes the guiding light toward a brighter, more resilient self.

Self-care in the context of relationship closure encompasses a multifaceted approach. It starts with acknowledging the emotional impact of the breakup and giving ourselves permission to grieve. This involves accepting the wide range of emotions that may surface, from sadness and anger to relief and confusion. Self-compassion is the cornerstone of self-care during this time, as it allows us to be gentle with ourselves and recognize that healing is a gradual process.

Nurturing physical well-being is another vital aspect of self-care. Eating a balanced diet, getting regular exercise, and ensuring adequate sleep are essential components of maintaining physical health. These practices not only contribute to our overall well-being but also boost our resilience and emotional stability.

Self-care also involves creating a supportive environment. This may include surrounding ourselves with friends and loved ones who offer comfort and companionship. Sharing our feelings and experiences with trusted confidants can provide emotional release and validation. Or, depending on the person, self-care can mean spending time alone, exploring inner thoughts and journaling. Each person's self-care should be tailored to their personality and needs.

Engaging in activities that bring joy and relaxation is integral to self-care. Pursuing hobbies, exploring new interests, or simply taking time for self-indulgence can be therapeutic. These activities serve as reminders that life is rich with experiences beyond the scope of the relationship.

Mindfulness and meditation are powerful tools for self-care and healing. These practices promote self-awareness, emotional regulation, and stress reduction. By staying present in the moment and cultivating self-compassion, we can navigate the emotional landscape of the breakup with greater ease.

Healing, in the context of relationship closure, is an intricate process that varies from person to person. It involves acknowledging the pain and trauma of the past, seeking professional support if needed, and gradually rebuilding a sense of self. Healing also means reframing the narrative of the relationship's end, emphasizing personal growth and resilience gained from the experience.

Forgiveness, both of the other person and ourselves, plays a pivotal role in healing. Forgiveness is not an erasure of past wrongs but a conscious choice to release the emotional burden of resentment and anger. It is an act of self-liberation that fosters emotional healing.

Self-care and healing underscore the profound importance of prioritizing one's well-being in the wake of a relationship's end. It speaks to the resilience of the human spirit and the transformative power of self-compassion and self-care. Healing is a journey of self-discovery and growth, leading toward a future filled with renewed strength and the potential for healthier and more fulfilling connections.

Conclusion

In coping with the end of a relationship, it is imperative to underscore a profound truth that encapsulates the essence of this entire journey: the hard work of healing, detaching, and moving forward is ultimately for oneself and has the transformative power to reshape one's life in remarkable ways.

Throughout this book, we've explored the intricacies of releasing attachments to people, navigating the complexities of relationships, setting boundaries, processing grief and loss, and the importance of self-care and healing. In action, the recurring theme has been that the path to detachment and healing is not only an act of self-preservation but also a profound act of self-love and self-empowerment.

The effort invested in understanding healthy relationships, recognizing toxic patterns, and seeking support is not merely a reaction to external circumstances but a conscious choice to reclaim one's sense of self and well-being. It's about realizing that the end of a relationship, even if painful, can serve as a catalyst for personal growth and transformation.

The act of setting boundaries is an assertion of one's worth and autonomy. It communicates a message to oneself and others that self-respect is non-negotiable. It is a step towards self-empowerment that lays the groundwork for healthier connections in the future.

Processing grief and loss is a deeply personal journey that, when undertaken with self-compassion and resilience, can lead to newfound strength and emotional growth. It involves not only acknowledging the pain but also recognizing the potential for personal insights and transformation that can emerge from the process.

Moving forward is an act of courage and self-discovery. It's about rekindling one's passions and pursuits, reconnecting with one's authentic self, and setting new goals that align with personal values and aspirations. In the process, individuals often find a deeper understanding of themselves and their desires.

Self-care and healing are the cornerstones of this transformative journey. They are affirmations of self-worth and self-love. When we prioritize our own well-being, we not only heal from the wounds of the past but also emerge as more resilient, self-aware, and emotionally mature individuals.

The hard work of releasing attachments to people is, above all, a labor of love for oneself. It is an acknowledgment that each person has the capacity to heal, grow, and thrive independently. The process of detachment and healing has the transformative power to reshape one's life, not only mending the wounds of the past but also preparing the individual for a future filled with healthier, more fulfilling connections and a deeper sense of self. It is a testament to the enduring resilience and potential for personal growth that lies within each of us.

www.ingramcontent.com/pod-product-compliance
Lightning Source LLC
Chambersburg PA
CBHW060910260726
48661CB00008B/3567